Shallow Depths

By: Richard Jennings

Dear Reader,

Thank you.

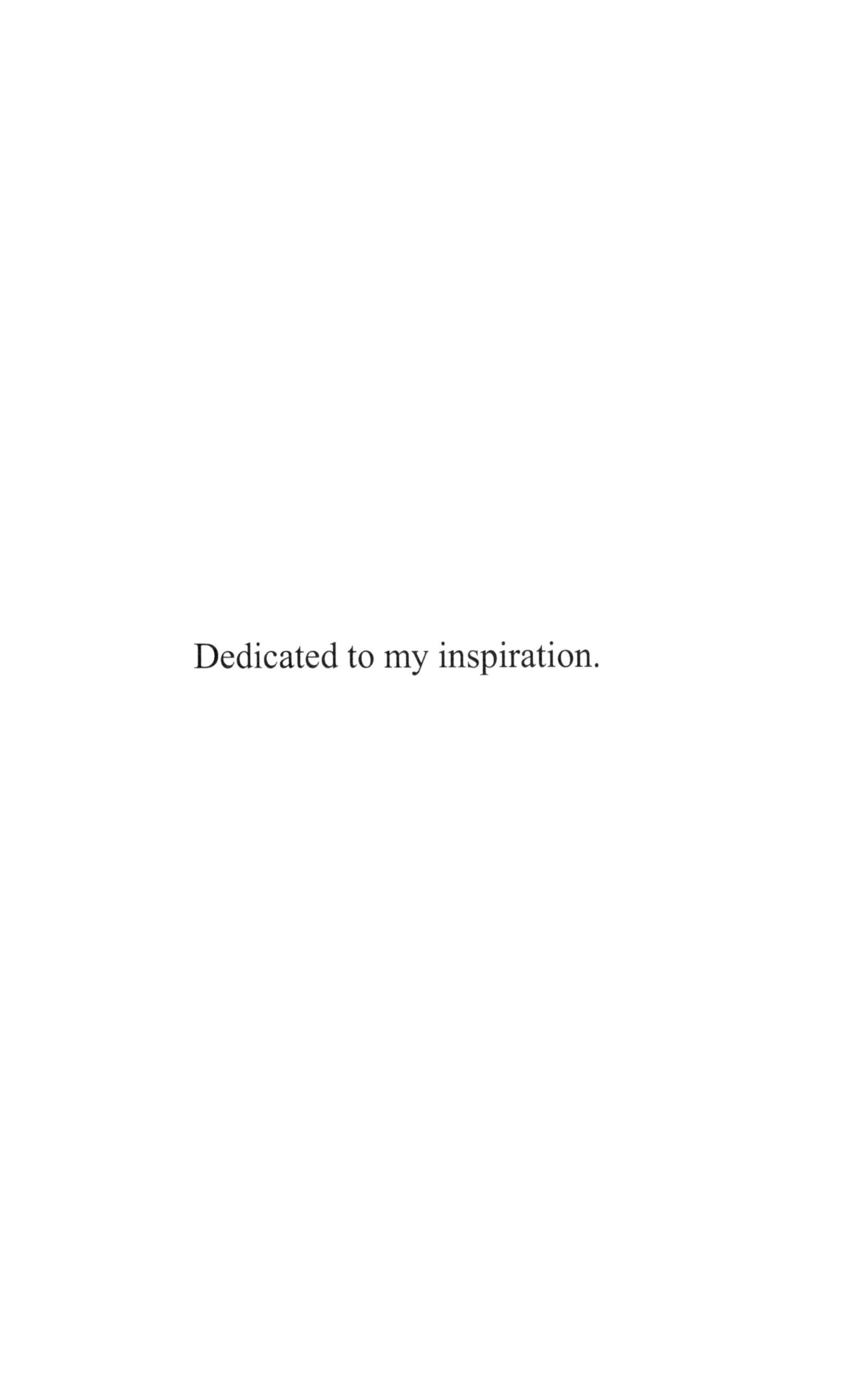

Dedicated to my inspiration.

A Good Night at Work

It was a regular Monday night when you came. Turns out you had forgotten my name. You said I look like a Matt. What's up with that? It doesn't really matter though, because I didn't get the chance to flatter you. You were the best thing about that Monday night. I could've only wished to behold such a beautiful sight. I wish I had the courage to tell you my thoughts. I wish I were braver but I'm not. So forgive me if I act a little weird. I only wish to see you smiling ear to ear. My affection for you runs deeper than the Nile. Se let me be the source of your smile.

Alliteration Outrage

I am the lonely loner loathing love
Sadly searching somewhere for a sign from above
Riff raff rhymes repeated rapidly
Alliteration overload attended to avidly
But beware bad beats biting back
Tied to teeth tongue twisting attack
Lonely loner leaving lovers lost
Faking feelings leaving fictitious futures feeling false
Legitamite loser losing at losing loudly
Praying for peace played on a propped up pride
proudly
A literal alliteration laceration lacerated libidos
leaving egos beaten and bloodied badly
While leaving lovers twistedly tongue tied with a
tough time trying to repeat a rough rhyme of mine
line for line puckered up like lemon lime losing their
minds in an outdated outrageous outrage of overtime
Say you can say sick shit like I said and twisted
tongues will lie dead trying to do what I did

And it's So Hard (Self Control)

She's lying next to me.
I'm staring at the ceiling.
And it's so hard not to put my arm around her.
It's almost killing me not to.
Because I feel like I've got to.
And it's so hard not to put my arm around her.
And she moves closer.
But I'm not moving over.
And it's so hard not to put my arm around her.
My heart beats fast.
My breath doesn't last.
And it's so hard not to put my arm around her.
How I feel I'm sure she knows.
But for her my feelings grow.
And it's so hard not to put my arm around her

Back Stabber

And again I'm forced to sit back and grit my teeth
As you twist the knife you've plunged so deep
Into my back when it was turned
As I was watching the bridge that you just burned

I thought you were my friend
But I was wrong in the end
Because you did it even though
You knew that it would hurt me so

I really should've known
For all the signs you've shown
So I'm closing all the doors
You're no friend of mine anymore

It's nice to know you're just a back stabber
But I appreciate the knife
Because you could never kill me
No matter how hard you try

Behind the Poker Face

When the chips are on the table the game tends to change
People play differently even though the cards are the same
Play your hand close to your chest
Put on your poker face hide your thoughts from the rest
Think again when you think you've thought enough
All in again to call the bluff
Put the cards on the table and do it or let it die
And the winner's decided in the blink of an eye
But I won't tell you who won, that's too much information
Instead I'll leave you with a confusing sensation
Because I'm sick, sadistic, and just a little twisted
Trying to catch myself, but I already missed it
Evasive, persuasive, and downright invisible
I must admit I'm a strange individual
My thoughts are all over the place
Hidden behind my poker face

Believe In Me

Have faith in me
It can go a long way
If you believe
I'll close the gap today
The distance between us
It means nothing to me
Just believe in me
You will see
As I carry on
If you have faith
No matter how hard
I will have the strength
Unwavering
Never faltered
I carry on for you
I am never halted
But I can't do it alone
I need you to see
That I need you
To believe in me

Bleeding Rose

Would a Rose, by any other name
Not smell as sweet?
But what happens
When the Rose begins to bleed?
The White Rose
Exposed to love
Is not the Rose
Exposed above
The White Rose
Isn't White in the end
It wants to show love
So it turns itself Red
It gives so much
That it begins to bleed
Nothing in return
To replenish what it needs
So the White Rose Red
Bleeds more blood than it has
So the White Rose Red
Bleeds to Black
Would a Rose, by any other name
Not smell as sweet?
But what of the Black Rose
Lying at your feet?
So take this White Rose
And give me the love that I need
Before the Red Rose
Begins to bleed
I love you
So love me back
Before this Rose
Bleeds to Black

Burning My Guitar

I'm sitting by a fire
On a lonely summer night
Singing to you so sweetly
And everything's alright

But I come back
From my head
The memories
I can't forget
Of me and you
The things we did
And I'm not sure
I can handle it

You left me sitting all alone
By a heart made out of stones
With a fire still inside
Burning
Keeping love alive

That's why I'm burning my guitar
I'm giving up on music
I'm not sure now who you are
But I'll never do what you did

That's why I'm burning my guitar
I'm not sure now who you are
Throw it in the fire we built together
It was supposed to burn forever
It was supposed to burn forever
It was supposed to burn forever
But now it's burning out

You left me there that summer night
My heart says this just can't be right
You'll come back to me somehow
But my head is heavy
Full of doubt

I hope and I pray
For the rise of the day
When you'll see my face
And your heart will race

But you left me sitting all alone
By a heart made out of stones
With a fire still inside
Burning
Keeping love alive

You left me sitting all alone
By a fire in a heart of stones
Will the flame burn on
When my guitar is gone?

So I'm burning my guitar
I'm gonna test my theory
Will the fire still burn on?
And will you ever hear me?

I will never play again
I'll never sing another song
But that's only if
The fire won't burn on

Burning

The addiction's getting stronger
I'm beginning to lose control
I can't handle the heat
And it's burning my soul
Your love is a fire
Burning my heart
Right from the start
With the power of truth
I fall in love with you
Your fire is giving me chills
Testing my power of will
Tempting me to do wrong
With a power so strong

Call Me Maybe, Baby

Call me maybe
I can call you baby
I can whisper in your ear
Anything you want to hear
I can hear the voices
Calling your name
See the pieces
Playing your game
But call me baby
Call me tonight
I can make you
Feel like you're alright
So pick up the phone
I'm here alone
I'll answer for you anytime
I've got nobody on the other line
So call me maybe
I can call you baby

Change

Listening to some silly love songs
Wondering how it could be so strong
And feeling like I'm invincible
Remembering when I was invisible
And I can't help but to smile
At how after a while
Things changed
Like they always do
The only thing that's the same
Are the eyes I see through
And I can see so much
But it's all such a blur
Like the way things are
And the way that they were
Like the kid that I used to be
When everyone was using me
And I'm not saying names
But I'm glad that things changed
Because I'm better off now
Without you in my life
The only reason I'm alive
Is because you didn't have a knife
But I got over it
Forgave and forgot
But look at me now
See how far that I've got

I've got real friends
And people that love me
And I'm on top
Nothing but the sky above me
I'm the king of the world
And I'm loving every minute
I love where I'm at
And everybody in it
But it wasn't always great
I started off slow
Back in the days
Before I had a phone
When I used to play outside
With a two way radio
Walkie talkie kid
That's how I was known
But that changed too

Now that I'm grown
And it doesn't matter now
How things were before
Because I changed for the better
Better than before
Because I used to be a ghost
The kid that no one knows
The weird kid
The one in the corner
Nobody talked to me

I was a loner
I was far from cool
And I tried my hardest
But it was the others
Who made it the farthest
I never got to be cool
Because my style wasn't the loudest
But I'm better off
I'm no longer an outcast
I've got a clique now
Of kids just like me
Who have my back
When kids try to fight me
But I guess we're not kids
Not so much anymore really
We're getting pretty old
And we're making our own theories
But we're better off
Things changed for us
We used to be some kids
Who were straight out of luck

But things changed
And I'm glad they did
Because I love the way things are
It's better than how they've been
Because I wasn't always happy
I couldn't always smile

And even nowadays
It's only once in a while
But happiness is fleeting
And so is the charm
I'd use it more often
But it only does me harm
I end up with situations
Predicaments of dedication
Decisions I'm not ready to make
Chances I'm not ready to take
But things change
They always do
The one thing I thought would last forever
Well that one's changing too
So as time carries on
Who are we to say no
We just let it guide us
On the way so slow
But no matter what happens
One things stays the same
The only perfect constant
Is that things always change

Classroom Blasphemy

Science teacher said love is just a chemical reaction,
but I know it isn't true
Love is so much more than that, I know, because I
feel it for you
And the things you do
And I had to tell
The teacher to go to hell
Because love is not an equation
Love is a journey and a destination
It's not some formula
That he can cook up
Love is much more than they're telling you
Love is blasphemy in the classroom

Collateral Love

The clock is ticking away
Second by second I lie awake
Checking my phone to see your name
Waiting for a message that never came
I make mistakes because I'm only human
But my greatest one was not letting you in
And I have no regrets in this story I tell
Except before I was ready, you already fell
I thought I knew the damage love could do
Until I spent so long away from you
So if you want to know the truth
When you fell for me, I fell for you
And now I know the meaning of pain
A thought as persistent as the rain
You, you're stuck in my head
You, when I go to bed
You, when I wake up
You, and the break up
But you say you still love me
And though I can't see
I still believe
In what we could be
And to let you in, and tell the truth
That I'm sure you know, I still love you too

Crying

Tear drops fall like rain, crashing to the ground
I call out your name, but you're not around
I look for you, but all I can see
Are the tears like rain, crashing at my feet
I cry, every night
Do I, have the right?
Or, is it reserved for
The broken hearted
Whose love departed?
I cry
I cry
Every night
For, me and you but
Crying's not what, I should do but,
I can't help myself from, thinking about you, love
And I cry
I cry
Every night
People cry sometimes
Because of lies sometimes
Or broken hearts from
The ones they once loved
But I can't tell you why
I cry
I cry
Tear drops sliding down the window pain
Like rain, rain drops falling softly down my face
Every night
I cry

I cry for you
And, I cry for me too
I look around and all I can see
Are tears like rain, crashing at my feet
And I keep crying
And I keep crying
Every night
And the tear drops fall like rain

Deny the Downfall

I'm strong enough to fight
And smart enough to learn
Everything I've got
I'm willing to burn
But there's one thing
I won't give up
It's the thing
I love too much
I promise
That it's true
I'm denying the downfall
Of me and you
I'll never give up
When it comes to us
I would give it all
To deny the downfall

Distance

I love you but you're so far away
I pray everyday just to see your face
The look in your eyes like a place ablaze
Tell me you love me and I'll be amazed
But the truth, of the fact, of the matter is
That no matter what, we can't handle this
Distance in your eyes between every kiss
Tearing at the corners of our only bliss

Double Edge (Duality)

Deep inside your mind
The feelings that you hide
They tell you not to be who you've become
But you can't stop you've only just begun

You are
Who you never knew
Who you
Could never be
And I love you

I'm not sure why
But I know you've changed
And things can never be the same

My heart says I love you
But my head is screaming no
I'm on the edge of a knife
I don't know which way to go

Loving you is killing me
But it's all that I believe
It's the only future I can see
Us together happily

But the way that you're acting now
I just can't see how
We could ever be that way
And I'm not sure what else to say

But I love you
Even though my heads screams no

It echoes my mind
I think about it all the time
The slightest difference
In you and I
Is this love or is it a lie?

I'm not sure why
But I know you've changed
And things can never be the same

My heart says I love you
But my head is screaming no
I'm on the edge of a knife
I don't know which way to go

Loving you is killing me
But it's all that I believe
It's the only future I can see
Us together happily

Embrace the Angel

The time has come for letting go
The angel waits with open arms
The time has come for goodbye
The angel means no harm
The angel comes
He comes for you
The angel comes
We shall miss you
In a different place
You shall thrive
Embrace the angel
And do not die
Embrace the angel
Forever alive
Embrace the angel
Goodbye

Remember we love you
We always will
We will never forget
The feel of the thrill
Of the life you had lived
And shared with us
Don't forget to forgive
For the wrong's you've been done
Embrace the angel
We love you
Embrace the angel
We will miss you
Embrace the angel
It's your time
Embrace the angel
Goodbye

Fallen Angel

Fallen Angel
From up above
I fell for you
I fell for love

Who could know
Love is a sin?
I got kicked out
Because I let you in

Even though I knew
That you didn't belong
I don't feel
That what I did was wrong

Have you ever felt
A love so strong
That you would sacrifice
The only place you belong?

That you would give it all up
And live with the choice forever?
But happy with it
Because you live together?

This is the feeling
This is love
This is the one thing
Worth falling from above

Fight for Your Life

Crack your knuckles
Get ready to win
Fight for your life
And you're going in
This could be it
Life could be over
But you're not done yet
Fight harder than ever
This could be the end of the line
But push the limits, it's go time
Break the barrier between life and death
Talk is cheap so save your breath
Action is loud when the director yells
Take your queue and live to tell
Prepare yourself for struggle and strife
As you prepare to fight, for your life

Fireworks

Sitting on a farm in a field
You being here makes me feel so real
Sitting next to you on the roof of a truck
Catching your heart by a stroke of luck
You take my hand so it doesn't show
Keeping it hidden because nobody knows
You lean your head on my shoulder sweetly
I look down and your eyes greet me
The fireworks start, reflected in your beautiful eyes
Their splendor can't compare to the beauty of you and I
Time passes slowly in the explosive bliss
And the finale comes, sealed by a kiss
Clapping and laughing as if for us
Everyone around starts getting up
They go for food to be merry and fattened
We follow suit as if nothing happened
But we both know the truth
The love between me and you

Free Period (Writer's Curse)

40 minutes to write
And nothing to write about
40 minutes to try
And figure something out
Music on
Pencil ready
Paper out
Rhythm steady
Content to write about nothing
Because even nothing is something
So the words slowly grace the page
And the smile never leaves my face
I love to write
It's what I do
With a pencil
For my thoughts to channel through
Day dreaming is in the job description
Thoughts to paper is the only prescription
Sometimes I write and I don't know what for
And sometimes I think
In the form of metaphor
Seeing things as they aren't
But what they are
With some practice
It's not that hard
Sometimes I see things next to me
And I begin to think in simile
Comparisons using like or as
So many of them it could drive you mad
Fight the insanity with a smile
But I'm not a fighter
I think too much
This is the curse of the writer

Girl in the Band

My girl's next to me
She's holding my hand
But I'm staring up at this girl in the band
Because she's the one that I've loved
Ever since I was young
And she's had my eye from the start
And the beating of my heart
Increase in tempo when she's around
Totally focused yet completely zoned out
But back to the situation at hand
Sitting with my girl staring at the one in the band
Wishing it could be different
And suffering because it isn't

Give and Go

You should know I give 100% for you
And if I said I give another 30 it's true
So please believe me when I say
I give everything and more everyday
It kills me, I know
But it's a pain I'll never show
For your sake alone
I suffer to the bone
I offer the shirt off my back
Thankful you didn't take it
Because there's a chill in the air
And it's left me shaken
But it's not cold
And you can't feel it
It's the chill
Of the realistic
The view I have
I can't handle anymore
But I still try to be better than before
It works, because I'm strong
But it fails in the long run
Because it kills me
The more that I give
Soon enough
I won't have enough to live
But until then I'll keep on giving
And I'll never stop
I'll keep on giving
Until the day that I drop
And even then
I will give from my knees
Until I am nothing
But dust in the breeze

Head Over Heart

I can't explain
I can't define
All of the things
I feel inside
And it's tearing me apart
Between my head and my heart
My heart feels the truth
But my head wants the proof
The reason why
I can't deny
The power held by
You and I
All the thoughts within my mind
And all my hopes for the rest of time
Come together when it comes to us
To form a storm made out of chaos
In the throes of our tomorrow's death
My heart refuses to take another breath
This goodbye leaves my head pounding
Pumping the blood for my heart, who's last breath still resounding
The final words of my love
Cursing those above
Because the love was too weak
That was given to you and me
And the heart lies still
With my mind going in for the kill
Love lying lifeless and cold
The lies of the story I told
The feelings I thought I felt
The truth is the blow of death that I dealt
And I didn't mean to
Because I want to love you

Here for You

This one's coming from way down deep
It's about the reason that I can't sleep
I decided to write you a poem
To say that I'm not in pain I'm just alone
I hate waiting when I'm confused
Especially when there's nothing that I can do
Because I hate it when you're not okay
And I can't stand when you're in pain
I can't help it and I can't help myself
From wishing there was some way I could help
But I will never go astray
I'll be here for you forever starting today

Here with You

Everyone's going places but I feel like I'm stuck here
So if you want to look for me this is where you'll find me dear
I'm telling you now
I'm probably never getting out
But I'll be okay you see
As long as you're here with me
I can be invincible, as solid as the sky
We can be untouchable, they can't compare to you and I
Because nothing can last as long as our love
To infinity and beyond babe, vzhuru do nekonecna

Hold My Hand (Extended)

Hold my hand
I'll sing you a sweet song
I'll wipe the tears from your eyes

So hold my hand
I'll tell you what you want to hear
Even if it's only lies

They may only be words but they're all we have
Holding us together in the shifting sands
But we're torn apart and we're not alright
So baby please, hold my hand tonight

Hold my hand
Maintain the image
Make people think that it is what it isn't

Because we haven't been happy in so long
And it's obvious we don't belong
So it's time to go our separate ways
But first let's give it a few days

Because we could be wrong
But we could be right
So baby, hold my hand tonight

We'll tell everybody what they want to hear
We'll keep a smile from ear to ear
Hiding what we really feel
They'll never know what's really real
Nothing but smiles between me and you
But deep in our eyes is a different tune
So hold my hand, connect me to you

Hopes and Dreams

Our dream of the sunset on the rock at the creek
The bitter distance between you and me
The things that make our story so tragic
And those that make it so magic
The dreams we have and hold
The lies we swore we never told
The things we said we would do together
Relying on our love lasting forever
As far as I'm concerned it will
Because I will love you even when my heart lies still
I clutch tightly to the dreams that we've come to know
They're the heart of the love that I can't let go
The dreams that we held so dear for so long
They're what keeps me up crying, but holding on
Missing our hopes and dreams kills me inside
But saying I didn't enjoy it would be a lie
Because I still dream our dreams
I still hope our hopes
I'm holding on
Tearing at the seams
But I'm never letting go
I'm holding on
Our hopes and dreams are what keep me going
Even when you're not here to hold when it's snowing
They keep me going even when I can't
And they'll keep me clutching even after the end
Holding on to you and me
Holding on to our hopes and dreams

I Live For Others

Let's be honest, I should be dead right now
And the question on everybody's mind is how
My dad died in May of 2008
I was supposed to with him in the truck that day
I was supposed to die by his side
But I got lucky enough to survive
My reasons for living are much too strong
I live for others, and I've lived for too long
I've died a thousand times, and then some
And I'll die a thousand more before my day is done
And when the sun sets, what will you say?
Will you be able to say that I didn't die in vain?
Because I live for others, I always have
It's the only reason I didn't die with my dad
Don't cry, I don't want you to
I only want to know the truth
I live for others; it's all I know how to do
But did I die in vain when I died for you?
The answer is most likely a yes
And I hope it makes you second guess
Because the truth is that nobody deserves me
And none of you even had to earn me
I gave myself of my own free will
And I hope this fills you up with guilt
Because I died for you, over and over again
And I keep coming back for you in the end
But soon enough the time will come
When my day is truly done
And I will die for you one last time
Will you be able to look me in the eye?
And will you be able to honestly say
That I didn't die in vain?

I'll Eat These Words

Silently screaming my heart out because it doesn't want to be with me anymore. Tearing myself apart because I'm falling through the door. I suppose this is goodbye, but I won't wipe the tear from my eye. I kind of like the torture I feel, and this is just a poem it's nothing real. These words are only words with no meaning between them. But before the night is through I might be forced to eat them.

I can't take the pain, sitting alone in the rain. On the porch of an empty place dreaming of the last time I saw your face. I don't know why I act like I don't care. I don't know why I act like I'm okay when you're not there. The truth is I can't face the truth of the situation. But the thought of acceptance leads to aggravation. I deny the fact that I'm not alright. I sit back and put up a fight. These words are only words with no meaning between them. But before the night is through I might be forced to eat them.

I'm No Hero

Don't call me a hero
It's farthest from the truth
I'm not the good guy
I'll leave that to you
I'm just the guy
At the right place and time
I had a stroke of luck
And left somebody awestruck
But I'm no hero
No, I'm no hero
So don't call me one
I'll even say please
Because when you lie with dogs
You end up with fleas
And I'm the worst of all
I watched many a downfall
And didn't lift a finger
To help or to hinder
I remain apathetic
To the world so pathetic
I don't care for antics
I don't fight for the frantic
I'm only a man
Too drunk to stand
Don't call me a hero
I'm no hero

In a Song

I left my heart between the notes, of the melody that I wrote, for you on that summer night, right before we had the fight, that tore our world apart, and stopped our beating hearts. We've forgotten how to feel, and we're not sure what's real. We think we know but we're always wrong. And we're not sure if we love each other anymore because it's been so long. But I can assure you that even though I've left my heart in this song, I only think of you when I'm gone. So between the notes of the melody, you can find the music far ahead of me. I fall behind, not keeping time, because you're too heavy on my mind. So even though we fought about it, we could never live without it. We still love each other, missing one another. But whenever you feel lonely when I'm gone, just remember that I put my love for you in the notes of a song.

Invalid Introduction

Introductions are invalid
Because everybody already knows
But they don't remember
Because I am a ghost
Hopelessly devoted
To going unnoticed
The face of a forgotten name
The outcome remains the same
You seem to have forgotten me
In the wake of this monotony
So here I am
The forgotten man
To remind you once again
To see if you'll remember then
But you might not
The face that you forgot
A picture too faded to fix
The memories you'll never miss
So I let the introduction go
To a person I already know

Killing Me Slowly

It's been so long
And
You're so far away
That
I can't tell
If
You're okay
And
Its killing me slowly
Today
And I can't handle
The pain

Kiss Me

The way to my heart is through my lips
So if you want me, give me a kiss
Don't be afraid to let me know
You've got to be brave and let the feelings show
Actions always speak louder than words
So let me know how you feel with yours
Because if you don't show me, I'll never see
And then we'll never know how it could be
So before you get the chance to miss me
Go ahead and kiss me
Use my lips as a telephone
To tell my heart it's found a home
Your lips to mine
Becomes a direct line
So lead the way to bliss
And give my heart a kiss

Life Decisions

I'm just a kid trying to find his way in life
But it's all just balanced on the edge of the knife
This way or that way I can't decide
But either way I'm gonna fall and I can't lie
I like the way that it feels
Because the pain is helping me deal
With the choices that I can't face
The obstacles of every day
Life isn't that hard but kind of confusing
Taking advantage of the things we've been using
But I've got to decide what I want
Where to go to college and what not
Trying to get a job and all that
And maybe even blog in all caps
When it comes crashing through
Venting about deciding what to do

Lonely Moments

Sipping hot chocolate out in the cold, I always think of you on days that it snows. The hood of my car never felt so empty, as it does now without you next to me. I feel cold, but not because I am. I feel cold because you're not holding my hand. A part of me is missing. It's gone so far away. But I know it's safe with you, wherever you may stay. So keep me safe, and hold me close. Until today becomes tomorrow. So never let go, and keep me warm. Until the day that summer comes.

Love is Murder

You'll hear no noise from me as the tears stream down my
face
You'll hear no noise from me as a sign of my pain
Because I'll suffer and you'll never know
Yeah I'll suffer and it'll never show
Because more often than not my tears are the only ones to
kiss me goodnight
And especially so on those nights like tonight
When all I can think about is you
And not being able to love you like I'm supposed to
And it's tearing me apart
Because inside the depths of this beating heart
There's a picture of you and me
To represent what love should be
But it's secretly killing me every time
I can't take your hand in mine
Loving you is murder in the first degree
Because loving you, is killing me

Midnight Sun

It was midnight, and the sun was shining. My soul was happy, and I was smiling. She had said yes, and she had kissed me. It seemed like the lord had truly blessed me. But back to the beginning, to the nonsensical sinning. A midnight sun illuminating love. She is truly a gift from above. But how could the sun shine during the night? And how could this nonsense feel so right? But it's all okay; we'll wait for the day. Maybe it will be dark. But it won't hide your heart. We can be together as one, under your heart, the Midnight Sun.

Music and a Girl

Nodding my head as I carry on
With my head phones in, the world is gone
People are talking but I can't hear
The problems of the world have disappeared
I don't have a care in the world
As I listen to a song about a girl
Thinking of the one I love
Giving thanks for the gift from above
Her and music is all I need
The rest of the world can let me be
Because I'm happy, and I quite don't care
About the negativity in the world out there
I've got my music and my girl
And I don't have a care in the world

My Angel

Fortify my soul with a smile
Rest your heart on my shoulder a while
Let it be my angel for a bit
Because my love for you will never quit
But a conscience isn't allowed through the door
Because all is fair in love and war
So the angel that guides
My decisions lies
Because I fight not for the good above
I fight for the glory of love
And violence showing passion puts me on top
Forever and always because the fighting never stops
So rest your heart on my shoulder
I'll move the unmovable boulder
I'll take the weight of the world from your back
I'll make up for the strength that you lack
I'll show you what my love could do
I'll carry on the fight for you
I'll show you beauty from every angle
If you'll only be my angel

My Miracle Pill

Just another day
Another waking moment
A piece of the pain
Need someone to hold me
Recover from the cuts
Ease the past
Get the guts
The courage to ask
I want her to be mine
I wonder if she will
My pain killer
My pill
But she's more than that
This I know
At the drop of a hat
I would show
Smiles she makes
Smiles she causes
Don't hesitate
No time for pauses
Look her in the eye
Let her see my soul
Put together the pieces
Make me whole
I know she could
But I wonder if she will
Maybe she would
My miracle pill

Need to Talk

All I wanna know is what's so wrong with us, and why are we so messed up? That we can't even see the truth, the distance between me and you. And we act, blind to the fact, that the past is never coming back. But if there's to be a future for us, we can never give it up, or risk losing our only forever, the promise we made to be together. So call me, when you get the chance. Call me, when you want. Call me, when you can. Call me, because we really need to talk.

You already know the number, you already know the name. So call, and ask for me, the voice you won't believe, when I repeat, you're beautiful from your head down to your feet. And I'll say again, if you really want, what I've been saying all along. So call me, when you get the chance. Call me, when you want. Call me, when you can. Call me, because we really need to talk.

And if you don't get the point by now, you should call me, so I can tell you. So I can tell you I love you, in every different way. I can tell you I miss you, every single day. Call me so I can tell you how I feel, and how you make me real. Call me so I can tell you, everything I already have, and I'll always tell the truth, over and over again. So I'll be waiting to give you my all, by the phone, for a phone call. So call me, when you get the chance. Call me, when you want. Call me, when you can. Call me, so I can sing you a love song.

Not, Won't, Am.

I could cry, but I'm being brave. I could cry, about yesterday. I could lie, but that's just not my way. I could lie, and tell you I'm okay. But I'm not the lying kind. Not that state of mind. So instead I write to you. Telling you what I could to. But I won't. I won't. I won't cry; I'm being brave. I won't lie, it's not my way. I won't cry, about yesterday, and then lie, straight to your face, as I say I'm okay, but I'm not. So instead I write to you. Telling you what I could do. Telling you I'm not. Telling you I won't. Even though I am.

Object

It's addicting
The sight of it
I can't look away

Arms crossed
Legs tapping
Keeping the pace

Similarities between us
Not so different
She and I are

I can't help
Looking at her
Object of my desire

One and One Makes 2am

It's two in the morning but I'm still thinking about you
For some reason I can't sleep without you
Waiting for your name to grace my phone
With the words to say that you're coming home
And I know it's a long shot
But the hope is all I've got
And the thought of the odds is killing me
So if you'll take the chance to really see
My dedication to the words
The promise that you heard
That I will never give
Up the chance to live
Happily forever
One and One Together

Plucking Petals

She loves me
She loves me not
Maybe
But it's a long shot
She could
She might
Does she?
It feels right
Do I love her?
I think I do
She might
Or might not love me too
But if she's listening
Maybe somehow
Maybe she's thinking
Of me right now
I want her to know
That I love her dearly
I can not wait
Until she is near me
Maybe she is like me
Thinking these things too
And maybe she is like me
Plucking petals beneath the moon

Rage and Regret/Fire and Ice

There's a war of fire and ice raging in my head. Rage and regret. Rage and regret. Two forces of evil of devastation equal. Rage and regret. Rage and regret. Fear I can not face, and lies I can not tolerate. Why do I stand by, pretending not to die? Why do I not cry, as it kills me on the inside? There's a war of fire and ice raging in my head. Rage and regret. Rage and regret.

Rain Writing

I should be asleep, but I'm awake for the rain. And the writing is the only way to ease the pain. Tapping the glass as it falls. Continuously like the voice in my head as it calls. I should be asleep, but I'm awake for the rain. And the writing helps to ease the pain. Your voice in my head keeps me breathing. But I'm unsure because seeing is believing. It's been so long since I've believed. I can't help but wonder if I'm being deceived. But I love you. I always have. I love you as much as a lover can. I love you, and I always will. Even if I forget how to feel. I will always love you, and your name. Even if it keeps me awake, writing about the rain.

Rhymes

Don't rationalize it
It's still a crime
To write a poem
That doesn't rhyme
Even if the schemes are off
If it rhymes then that's enough
But if it doesn't
It becomes a mess
If no line
Matches the rest
And even worse
If it has no meaning
Then it's crap
From the beginning
So be careful
And watch yourself
Or you will lose track
Of your literary health

Scarred Heart

Putting holes in the walls inside me
Soon you'll see what I've been hiding
My heart bleeds so sweetly
It's such a rush
My heart keeps bleeding
I care too much
But not about you
But that's not the truth
I'm moving on
Because I have to
Your love is gone
But I don't believe you
I think you still love me
But it's hard to see
Because you didn't tell me much
About what you think and such
So I don't know what's going on in your head
And it bothers me when I lay down for bed
I think too much when I'm alone
Feeling the pain down through all of my bones
Still talking to your best friend
Helping her out with her problems
I still want to talk to you
But it would be awkward to
I wish you would talk to me
But things might never be
The way they were before
Because we're not together anymore
And I wish it wasn't true
Because I was happy with you

Scout's Honor

It's just another obstacle in our way
But we can make it if we take it day by day
I'm not sure yet what I should do
But together I know we can make it through
There's no power like the power of will
Enforced again by the strength of skill
Words I hope might be enough
But if not we've always got our love
Scout's honor, I'm making you a promise
To be strong for you, but I'll be honest
I'm no superman, I'm a zero
But for you I'll play the hero
And if it seems like more than you can take
I can kiss away all of your pain
And when you think you've had enough
Please, don't give up
You can borrow my strength
I'll carry us the entire length
This is the promise I'm making
This is the vow that I'm taking
We can do this
Scout's Honor

Shine Through For Me

Sleep won't come easy to a restless mind
So I'll never be at peace with one like mine
I'm as clouded as the sky on a stormy night
Waiting for the sun to shine through and set things right
But the clouds are thick and black
And I can't keep from looking back
The sun used to shine all the time
But now I can't seem to smile
The rain turns to steam as it hits my burning skin
I'm finding it hard to let you in
I know you are the light I've been looking for
But I can't seem to find the key to the door
So please, I want you to stick around
And if I can't open the door, please knock it down
Save me from the cover of this shroud
Let your light shine through the clouds
And see what no one has in a while
And look me in the eye as we share a smile

Sliding

You can stake your claim on my heart all you want
But I removed the flag that you fly when you flaunt
Because there's no better time than the here and the now
To let go of the lies that I have allowed
I can't let this go on anymore
My life slides away like a glass door
Transparency is all I can see
Because I see through you but you can't see me
So let me slide out of the way
Open the door that's keeping you safe
Because in my head your voice is residing
And all of those lies are the reason I'm sliding

The Essence of Happiness

I may be the king of sappiness
But you are the essence of happiness
The word in its purest form
The vision of beauty since you were born
And you are simply amazing to my eyes
I could never tell you a lie
You are perfection beyond belief
Negativity gives way to relief
You are my perfect hope of love
The one I call a gift from above
And I sit here loving you all the while
Silently speaking through a loving smile
You have killed me time and again
But I would die a million times and a million times ten
You are the sweetest of the sweet
The one I am so glad to meet
The smile never leaves my face
When we are in the same place
I want you to know that it's true
Every time I tell you I love you

The Haiku Haiku

The first and third lines
Have only five syllables
The second, seven

The Shame

You said it's not about the money
You said it's all about the heart
And all your words like honey
Had me blinded from the start
You see the greatest shame is
You only love me because I'm famous
But I mean it in a good way
So please listen when I say
That I know
You love the heart and soul
The ingredients of my music
Are what made you fall
As hard as you did
And I'd give it all
To hold you tonight
And set the world right
Because I miss you more than I can take
And it's broken me more than my heart can break
But I'll wait so long for you
And I'll sing these songs for you
But it's a shame that you're not here
And it's a shame that I'm not there
To hold you in my arms
Seduce you with my charms
But it's a shame we're so far apart
It's a shame you can't feel my heart
But I'll be home real soon
So I can make it up to you
And the greatest shame is
That I'm even famous

The Smile: The Veil

No one can see through the smile, the veil, the lie that I tell, while I cry, all the time, and it hides, deep inside. But I can't let you know, I can't let it show, and I can't let it go, for fear of losing control. Because I would break, worse than I already have. And it would take, all that I already am, and destroy me, or whatever's left. And show me, what I should have been. And I can't face that again, I can't face who I am. Who I've become, which of me won, this battle I was born to lose, this path I was forced to choose.

The Truth Flies on Forgotten Winds

Come back to my
Life like
Wax art
Sculptures
Beautiful
Max heart
I love
You know
The truth
Is hard to
Swallow
Flies away
On the wind
Of a forgotten page
Of a song sang When we
Made up
The words but
It hasn't happened
Yet and
It's my one regret
Because
Without the
Words
We can't seem to
Swallow
Can't fly
On the wind and
We'll never see
The truth
Of us
Being more than friends
And I just want
To be with you

Trip to the Groove

Clutching the cure I fade away
Slipping into the darkness of the day
Behind the music I hear a voice
My guardian angel to grant me a choice
But I'm not sure what I should do
The choice to make, the red pill or the blue
I made my choice because I wished to know
How deep the rabbit hole really goes

As the music fades the scene goes too
For some reason I have no shoes
I step out of bed into the sand
I think that I've reached Never Land
I end the trip with the sea at my feet
As I fade away into the beat

Remember kids that drugs are dangerous
And all kinds of crimes are heinous
But when you're feeling the flow and the music is smooth
Just turn up the volume and trip to the groove

Uncertainly Fun

Turn that frown upside down
Like you're flipping a switch
Your head is going back and forth
Like you're scratching an itch
Undecided and it's making you sad
But can not knowing really be that bad?
Maybe it's a good thing
To not know what to do
Uncertainty can be fun
But I'm uncertain if it's true
Either way it's worth the risk
So listen well to this
When the going gets tough
Do not run
You may find the challenge
Is uncertainly fun

Unread

For some reason I can't help but look at the girl next to me. Her voice is as soft as the way her hair falls so beautifully. She's astounding. Her voice is resounding, in my head long after she's gone. Please excuse me for rambling on. But I must confess, to the sight of her I can not protest. I doubt that I even cross her mind. I would talk to her more but I'm not the kind, who likes to make myself known. Writing is how my feelings are shown. But she will never read the words. I will never have the courage to show her.

Unspoken Story

I'm telling a story with the words that I can't seem to say
They seem so distant, like memories of a forgotten day
Unsure if I can find the words again
Or new ones with the same meaning in the end
But for now, I'll just sit here speechless
And somehow, I'll find forgotten reaches
Inside of my memory where the meaning lies
In wait to be spoken for the spark in your eyes
And a smile to grace your lips
And to be rewarded with a kiss
But those words are so hard to get to
So they may never reach you
But I will try to express
The entire extent
Of how I feel through actions and such
But I fear they won't be enough
So I sit here, thinking of some kind of token
To give you, instead of the words unspoken

Walls

I've built these walls inside my head
To hide the things I can't forget
Hiding them from everyone else
But mostly from myself
Who I am or used to be
Is hidden deep inside of me
And I can't get him out
Without some help
So give me a hand
And we can do well
To save him from his prison
The depths where he's been hidden
And reclaim who I'm supposed to be
The man who is supposed to be me
So it comes down to the two of us
Me, myself, and you
I built these walls with my own two hands
I'll tear them down with my own hands too

Warning Unheeded (How It Always Goes)
Close your mouth
Nobody cares
There's no importance
To the things you share
That's what they said
When the day was dawning
It's not my fault
They didn't heed my warning
Shut up
They said
Nothing but ignorance
In their heads
They told me
To keep to myself
But I didn't
I warned everyone else
And then they all fell
Like I said they would
But they didn't listen
When they could
They hated me
But it didn't matter
I'm here to warn
Not to flatter
But they admitted
All along I was right
That was that
It ended the fight
That's how it always goes
Why it does
Nobody knows
But their ignorance shows
I was right all along
And I've never been wrong

What Makes a Hero?

What does it take to be a hero?
What stops one from being a zero?
Do you need to be brave?
Do you need someone to save?
Or can it be anyone?
Who isn't afraid to run?
What makes a hero?
The things that they do?
Saving lives is great
That's true
But there are other things
That are pretty great too
Maybe it's something small
Like giving a smile
To someone who
Hasn't had one in a while
So tell me
What makes a hero?
And who can it be?
Can it be you?
Can it be me?
So tell me
What makes a hero?

Where's The Girl?

Where's the girl
I've been waiting for
Where's the girl
So I don't wait anymore
Where's the girl
Of my dreams
Where's the girl
Who's searching for me
Where's the girl
From the child's fable
Where's the girl
Sitting across the table
Where's the girl
I hold so dear
Where's the girl
She's right over here

Who I Am

I take solace in the center of my troubled mind
My head is racing with my body far behind
Too many thoughts and I'm going to lose control
Trying to dig my way out of this six foot hole
Grew up too quick when I lost my father
But soon I traded one struggle for another
My inner demons know me way too well
Growing up inside of my outer shell
I'm trying my best to make things right
But I'm the one person I just can't fight
But there was a loophole I couldn't see
I failed to realize that this isn't me
This is a collection of the walls I've built around myself
Hiding the real me from everybody else
I almost forgot who I really am
But I'm not going to let it happen again
My mind and my hands are my only weapons
I'm ready to face whatever happens
It doesn't matter whether I win or lose
This is a battle I was forced to choose
Confident in knowing that if I fall
I went in and gave it my all
Staring down myself without a doubt
One of us won't be coming out
Who I am, who I was, and who I ought to be
Only one of use can be the real me
At the end, alone I stand
To tear down the walls and expose who I am

You'll See

You'll see that I could do it when it's done. You'll see soon enough that you were wrong. You'll see that I'm more than you thought. You'll see that I can give you what you want. Soon enough you'll see. You could really be with me. But what will you want? I would give you all I've got. But will you take it? We can make it. But it's all up to you. Tell me what you want me to do. You'll see if you open your eyes to the truth. You'll see that I did all this for you.

Your Best Friend

Who took you home when he left you in the dark?
Who healed the wounds of your aching heart?
Who took you out and spent every dollar?
Who would answer whenever you holler?
Who was the one to save your life?
Who was the one to help you sleep at night?
Who is the one who will pull you from the fire?
If the answer isn't me then you are a liar
I always gave you the very best of me
Always with no thanks necessary
By your side even when you're mad
The best friend that you'll ever have
To steer you clear when you go astray
As long as you never push me away
But if you don't see the light
Chances are that you just might
But I hope that in the end
You hold on to your best friend

The Story of The Hero and The Heroine,
The Breaker and The Broken,
But Most of All,
The Heart

Hail the Hero

All hail, All hail
The one that never failed
Whenever he was needed
The Hero always prevailed

All hail, All hail
The Hero of the story
He never wanted fame
And he never fought for glory

All hail, All hail
The boy that everyone knew
He made everyone smile
Every time they were feeling blue

All hail, All hail
The boy who had no weakness
But how could he have known?
No body could have foreseen this

All hail, All hail
The future about to come
Everyone's got their weaknesses
This Hero only had one

All hail, All hail
The events about to unfold
And heed the message of the story
The story about to be told

Hail the Heroin(e)

All hail, All hail
The Heroine, the drug
She completed the Hero
When the Hero never was

All hail, All hail
A very beautiful girl
According to the Hero
The most beautiful in the world

All hail, All hail
The one the Hero loved
He thought the Heroine was a gift
An angel from above

All hail, All hail
The Hero's greatest sin
The Hero would have given his life
To be with the Heroine

All hail, All hail
The words that were already said
The Hero would have given his life
And the Hero nearly did

All hail, All hail
The Heroine fell for him too
The story was coming together
There was nothing they could do

Hail the Heartbreaker

All hail, All hail
The Heroine loved the Hero
She fell in love with the boy
Who started as a zero

All hail, All hail
Time past and the Heroine changed
She used to love the Hero
But her heart was rearranged

All hail, All hail
The tragedy about to happen
She no longer loved the Hero
But she was still so happy to have him

All hail, All hail
She told the Hero the truth
He searched her for a sign
Hoping to find some proof

All hail, All hail
The Hero didn't find
What he was looking for
Of her love, there was no sign

All hail, All hail
The Hero began to break
All he ever did was give
But he took more than he could take

Hail the Heartbroken

All hail, All hail
The broken hearted boy
He was known as the Hero
The Hero of the story

All hail, All hail
The Hero began to cry
He gave more than he had to her
So much that he nearly died

All hail, All hail
The Hero began to break
The Hero's heart was strong
But it took more than he could take

All hail, All hail
The Hero had failed
He put his hopes in love
But found that the ship had sailed

All hail, All hail
The Hero finally fell
He was the victim of the story
The story he lived to tell

All hail, All hail
The Hero alone again
He survived his only weakness
But was never the same in the end

All Hail the Heart

All hail the Hero
Who started as a zero
All hail the Heroine
Who was the perfect poison
All hail the heartbreaker
Much worse than a life taker
All hail the heartbroken
Who fell for words unspoken
All hail the heart
Blinded from the start

All hail the Hero
All hail the Heroine
All hail the breaker
All hail the broken

All hail the fire
All hail desire

All hail, All hail
The heart that told a lie
Everyone wants to play the Hero
But not this time

Dear Reader

I would like to personally thank you for taking your time to read this, even if it was only a few poems, or maybe even just one. It still means a lot to me. I hope these poems have touched you in a way that only emotions can, and I hope you loved every second of it.

Sincerely,
Richard Jennings